Brief Bio

*Born in Chicago's 'Roaring Twenties' – '27 to be
Exact*
*This year – with any luck I'll be '90' – It is
an "aging fact"!*
*Tulsa, OK Become my Home on Reaching
Grade School Age*
*Acting Weekly on Children's Radio and
Ever on the Stage!*
Began Writing Poetry at a Very Early Age
*My Writings Ran to Verse – Sometimes
Better – Often Worse!*
*Grad of Tulsa Central High '45 –
Attended Tulsa U. Too.*
*A Brief Glimpse of Poetry Writing and
Publication-*
*Published First at Age 8 in a National
Children's Magazine called*
*Wee Wisdom- They notified Tulsa paper
– A feature story and picture followed.*

This Sadly led to a kidnapping threat and
Ransom Demand – the 'Lindbergh Case'
fresh In People's minds.
FBI Stepped in – all SAFE!   But the
Threat Had Left My Widowed Mother
Terribly Upset! Her Words to Me – 'I
Know You'll Never Stop Writing Poetry
But Please Don't Be Published Again,
Dear!
And, I kept that promise until after
Reaching My 80th Year
At this 'Ancient Age' I Continue to Write
Am Published to My Delight and FEEL NO
FEAR!

50 YEARS BEHIND THE FITTING ROOM DOOR

50 YEARS BEHIND THE FITTING ROOM DOOR

MAROLYN D. STOUT

This was FuN to Live
and write —
Hope you find
it FuN to Read !
Marolyn Stout
2018

Contents

Acknowledgments and Dedication

Special Thanks to my helpers
YAC Service-Learning Cyclones
Sharun Philip '18, Malavika Rajaram
'20, and Carmen Clay '74
Book Publication Facilitator,
Metropolitan Library System Teen
Librarian, Miss Elisabeth Wright
Cover Art by Rick George,
Metropolitan Library System

This book is dedicated to my Beloved
late husband, Bob and my two Ever-
Precious Daughters Suzy and Barby who so
Graciously Shared Me for over 50 years of
Laughter and Tears making this Book a
Reality.
My Appreciation too – To My Ever-
Inspiring "Store Child" Mary Beth.
May God Bless You All, Always

50 Years Behind the Fitting Room Door

Fall 2011-Retired at Long Last- Age 84
The Large Window Signs Hang Limply-
States Simply
'CLOSING STORE'
Worked on North May Ave. – A Half
Century It's True-
Question Most Often Asked? – Answer is
Now Known
At How Early an Age Was 'Fashion
Interest' Shown?
In my aging Blue -Veined Hand
I Hold an Old Photo – Once Quite
Grand-

Slightly Wrinkled – a Bit Faded – Worn and Bent

But then So Am I More than 8 Decades of Life Spent!

There I was the 'Future Fashionista' – Age Almost 4

Playing 'Dress-Up' In a Pose – As I chose to stand

Outside My Grandparents' Vine Covered Sunroom Door!

So Fashionably Outfitted 'Head to Toe'

My Felt Cloche Hat – An Elegant Chapeau!

A Fox Fur Scarf – Glassy Eyes on the Clasp!

An Elegantly Beaded Drawstring Bag I Hold it Close and Fast!

Freshly Polished White 'Mary Janes' – Worn

Inside Mother's High Heeled Lizard Pumps

Walk Carefully – Step Cautiously –
Remember –
No- No – No More Leaps – No More
Jumps!
Just Clickety Clack on Sidewalk or Floor
–

Never Dreaming What Lay Ahead – Both
Outfitting Fashionably and Shared Prayers
in 50 YEARS BEHIND THE
FITTING ROOM DOOR!
Now the Picture in Hand – My Little
Dress- With Matching Bloomer Panty
All the Rage in the '30's Depression Age'
Sadly, My Chunky Little Leg – One Day
Caused 'One Panty Leg Elastics' to Snap –
Give Way!
My ever smiling Irish Father
(Who Died Much too Young – I was only
8)
Gave me a 'Fashionable New Name'
To remain in My Heart Evermores –
I Wipe Away Tears

Remembering All Through the Years –
Once
He Called Me His
"Little Miss Droopy Drawers"!

Pictures

After 50 years plus

Little Miss Droopy Drawers
Now has Lived On Another Five Years
More!
Hitting Age 90 This year – 2017
Yes, I Am Keeping Score.
And Comparing pictures – Two –
There is my first week – Take a Peek
Seated in the window of the store
Looking out onto N. May Ave –
It is spring 1961 – The Month is March
The 'WomenAKINS' are there too
Just Not in the Shot – Sad But True!
And Then – The Final Weeks of the
Final Store – Just Before Locking Forever
That Very Last Door.
Lets a Closer Look Take
At the Changes I Made – The Hair Do
–
The Glasses – Circles Under The Eyes –

Wrinkles and Smiling Crinkles Too!
But One Thing Remained The Same –
Unchanged
The 'Ever Fashion Right' – Color Scheme
–

For I shall Always Team –
Black and White – Be it Day or Night"!
It Remains 'My Final Fashion
Exclamation'
Until I Succumb to 'Shades of Gray'
My Ashes on my Joyous
Cremation Celebration Day'!

Prologue

Thus, Before I Open the Door of
That Very First Store — Chapter One —
At Age 33 — You, the Reader, May
Question as did I — How Did It Ever
All Come To Be? A Little Girl —
Such as Me — 'Little Miss Droopy
Drawers'
Ending up Spending Fifty Years and More
On the Ave. Known as North May OKC
Both
Behind and In Front of so Many Beautiful
Fitting Room Doors? Early On I
Learned — as the saying goes — to Get Rid
of the 'Droopy Bloomers Woes' so I Pulled
Up My New Big Girl Panties and
Moved On. Graduated Tulsa Central
High School 1945 — On to Tulsa U —
Studying Radio Acting — Drama — Speech
—

*Education – All The Things I Really
Loved to Do! Had There Been A
Class offered in 'Paper Doll Fashion
Design' I would surely Have Been
Enrolled There Too! I acted weekly in radio
from the 6th
Grade Thru My College Years. Met
and Married My Darling Husband Bob,
A Returning World War II G.I. (at the
time
of His Death.) Married Just Over 60 years.
In 1961 – Precious Daughters – We Had 2
Suzy and Barby – School Age It's True.
Back in 1954 we had moved from 'T –
Town'
(Tulsa) to OKC- It became Our Home
Forever More!
I Taught – Speech – Creative Drama-
Sub-Deb – Charm and When Television
Came On the Scene- Eventually, I Was
There on your small Black and White
Screen and Finally in Full Color Too*

You Never Knew just what I Might be
selling you! Pitching Refrigerators and
appliances in my crisp Little Shirtwaist
Dress (My Sunday School Class Called
me
"The Poor Man's Betty Furness)
Nationwide
she was selling Refrigerators Too!
There was Furniture – Station Wagons
to carry The Brownie Troop and Dairy
Products
too- in the years Before. I Showed Fashion
For You to View! Working with Many
Organizations My neighborhood Methodist
Church – Brownie and Girl Scouts – The
PTA
My Chi Omega Sorority Alumni Group –
There
was Always Another Meeting – Something
I needed to Do! But on That day – a
chilly Mid – February Day 1961 All Was
About To

*Change – as were the next 50 years of My
Life – Today I say 'It was not mere
coincidence but another one of "God's
Incidents" for me – I believe it Was
Truly Meant to Be! I had Done a
Luncheon Program For My Church's
Womens' Society – the title – The Church
in Southeast Asia – I turned Down a
Ride Home With my neighbor as a couple
of Quick Errands I needed to Do –
slip around the Corner to a strip of
shops which in that Day was called
Far North May Ave – First I would stop
at Fines Foods – I Had opened my Coin
Purse – a loaf of Wheat Bread I Did
Need – that would be a Dime – 29 cents
for a
Pound of Regular Ground Beef – But if I
Chose 'Ground Round' It would Be 39
cents
As I weighed that decision and Knew I
Needed to stop at the Veazey Drug too-*

Rounding the Corner Suddenly on
the Sidewalk Ahead there comes into view
Heavy Cords – Welding Equipment and
the
open Door of a large vacant store – Two
Gentlemen came Quickly out the Door
to Call – Be Careful – Don't trip – Don't
Fall
and that was officially the Start of It All!
One Man Was the Welder – the other
a small older southern Gentleman who
said 'Darlin' I'm Puttin' In an Elegant
New Fashion Store with Wrought Iron
Fencing as part of its 'window decor' –
we chatted Briefly – He introduced
Himself – as I did too – I said I was
eager for His store as there was
nothing in 'Ladies – Ready – to Wear' (as
it was
called in that day) – Nothing further North
than Mayfair NW 50th and May – and
this was

Lakewood – NW 68th and May – His
store
would have Beautiful Lease Departments
But I said I must quickly move on as
My Daughters and Students would soon be
there
I was grateful I Had a Tuna Casserole
to shove into the Oven- For I Did Have a
PTA board meeting promptly at 7:00! The
Next Morning as I was noisily
Running the sweeper – I Heard the
Phone Ring – Those Days – only 1 kind
of
phone. – All numbers in one Book – Just
Know the Name – Open the Book and
Look
The owner of the soon – to – be – store
said
He Had decided He Needed me to BE
More – Than just a 'customer' in His
Store – as I was so well acquainted
in the neighborhood – he needed me

*Working in his store – Meeting and
Greeting as He unlocked the Door of that
Very First Store on 'Far North May'!
As you would Guess – I said 'Yes" and
making a new Plan for My Daughters and
Students Began and All Worked Out Well!
Fast Forward 2 weeks- March 1, 1961 –
Once again
I Rounded that Corner- Having walked
My
2 short Blocks from Home – My Very First
Day in Fashion on N May lay just ahead
–
only 1/2 block more to that very first store
–*

*A small sack lunch – Purse in Hand I
Glanced
Back Round to Check my stocking seams –
Gave
my little Girdle a Final Tug of Adjustment
and made mental note- tomorrow walk
in flats- carry those 3" heels – I Had*

chosen my outfit with care – the classic
Little Black suit and pearls – Apparently a
wise choice for in years to come
I remember hearing the phrase -"From Our
First Date Until our Last Breath
PEARLS!" And
I was a little Breathless and Whispered A
Prayer as I reached the Door
of that very first store Elegant and New –
6811 N. May Ave!

Chapter I

A Beautiful Store Opens Elegant and New Springtime – March 1961 Far North May Ave

I had been advised it would be wise to arrive an hour prior to the 'Grand Opening Hour' on that chilly but brilliantly sunny opening 'Opening Day'! The sign in the freshly washed window – WELCOME – mannequins in colorful springtime attire for all to admire. Large Baskets and Congratulatory Bouquets in shades of pink were set against a background of beige – freshly painted beige walls Louvered Fitting Room Doors – Newly laid beige carpet touches of white wrought iron in the windows too – All to lure the 'Sidewalk Window Watchers' In – For a closer OPENING DAY View! A large 'Gold Starburst Clock' hung just inside on the wall. As its hands arrived on the appointed Opening Hour – Now – at last – the 50 Year Fashion Story on N. May can begin to Unfold – Be Told as I recall it all to This Day! Be Warm – Be Welcoming – and Coffee would be served in Cups and Saucers from a Large Silver Tray! Thus, the 'Learning Process for the Fashion Novice' – Officially Began! The little southern gentleman – (who had ladies ready to wear' had employed me) and lease departments there were another 3! They retained their original store Locations, but wished to be part of this 'Far North May' – Fashion Innovation! There was an area of young Children's and Infants wear – Set apart – and In a corner Furs – Capes – Stoles – Mink and Fox jackets – 1 or 2 – But the Largest Lease space of all – had So Much to View! She decided not to retain her store on N. Western Ave – She had Hats – Veils and Blossom – Bedecked Easter Bonnets to view! Lacy and Rather Revealing Sleepwear and Lingerie too – Push-up Bras and Bikini Panties – Some Done in Black and Animal Print considered quite FUN in 1961! She sold sparkling stone-set costumes jewelry (Bling was a word not as yet even heard) Sheer seamed hose – 3 pairs to a box and Lush Leather Handbags by Milch. Her fragrances by Bergdorf Goodman brought women by the score into the store! Among them – Many of my friends and neighbors living so near May Ave. That day the hours fairly flew – So when the closing hour came – I felt a sudden wave of sadness and shame – No Ticket had I written – No garment had I sold – that kind Southern gentleman did not scold – He simply smiled and said "Darlin' don't worry- Tomorrow will be a whole new day"- So True for Day Two – a customer I had spent time with the day before had returned to further explore – to try on an outfit she had admired. She stood before a large mirror very Elegantly Attired – in All the store had to offer – Almost Head to Toe – for the full exciting effect I had added my new Black Patent Pumps – 3 inch heels – while I stood by in my Stocking Feet – On my shoulder her squirming Baby – wanting something to Eat – I found his pacifier and quickly 'plugged him in' – My southern gentleman saw it all gave me a quick nod and a grin! I'd always heard of 'Walking in Someone's Shoes' This Time it meant a Big Ticket – Happy Customer- Sleeping Baby – and Good News – Me even back in my own darling shoes! Pumps in Black Patent Leather – Always my favorite – Whatever the hour – the occasion – the season or the weather!

Chapter II

*Through the Eyes of the All Knowing
Mannequins 'Famous Firsts' They Did View I
Now Pass Onto You*

From that very first day of the elegant
fashion store opening on North May – There
were many sets of eyes watching our large
show window by night and by day! On the
outside looking in to see – there were
window watchers and window wishers –
noses pressed close to the glass – some driving
curbside would also slowly pass – some
writing a quote or making a sketch or note
committing to memory the latest in Fashion
Fun that soft and lovely springtime – 1961!

There were also those who never lost sight by day or by night – 24/7 outside or in – each simply bore the title of a window Mannequin'- and what Each Body Wore – I Learned that Responsibility Belonged to Me! As well as Balancing the Lease Departments in – Window Viewing Time – a Bit More of a Chore that turned out to Be-! And now this is how Other Responsibilities were Soon passed on to Me! when the 'Big Fashionista' brought in by 'the small southern gentleman' on March one- (yes, she was from 'Big D'- His entire store to oversee – so sadly – on "May One" she told him she was 'DONE' his store was too great a 'Thankless Job' to Run! – there seemed to be – 'no choice left but ME'! – the 'job' came my way – along with a $5.00 a week – raise in pay – from $50.00 to $55.00 dollars a week – 6 days of course! – Remember I earlier stated that at that time a loaf of bread could still be purchased for one dime! Back now to the mannequins – for the story is theirs to tell – they passed it all to me and as their 'Window Dresser' I came to know them Very Well you might say rather Intimately – as it fell to me – to remove ever so gently Arms or a Hand by Reason of the Change of Season – they might appear 'casually Elegant'- Maybe 'chic Sporty' or 'fashionably Grand'! I would come to realize that summer winter spring or fall the Mannequins Eyes Viewed it All! Some of their eyes appeared shiny – their eyeballs like colored glass – other eyes and lashes would be 'carefully painted on' never allowing a restful blink or to close or perhaps Headless or No Eyes at All – be it dusk or dawn! Sunlight or Spotlights by day and Flood Lights to softened Security Light that burned on all thru the night! Now, as to how our relationship began – as I dressed them – zipped, buttoned, and caressed them – smoothing in place every seam – pleat and hem, I somehow sensed the 'Fashion Tales' so much both Seen and Heard and though they could not Speak a Word I know it Seems

Absurd but soon I was to become Their Listening Ear! And now with this Book – together you and I can Explore – Wisdom – Wit – Lessons of Life as the 'Mannequins' eventually become 'WomenAKIN' Wise Ever More – both Behind and in Front of many a Fitting Room Door! Among the 'Famous Firsts' that I must mention – 'Easter Hats' and their 'No Return' policy was brought to my attention – as there was a March Easter that year – over and over these words I did hear – No Returns – No Exchanges – No Refunds on spring millinery (Easter Bonnets) after 'Easter Day'- Hats a must in that era – soft felt or shining straw – often blossom bedecked – finished with a touch of dotted or simple veil – these hats were considered 'seasonal wear – a Final Sale ' to return 'a spring chapeau' – one or two did try (one did even almost cry!) but alas, the rule held fast – it was All to No Avail! The second 'Famous First' I learned early on as the right 'Fashion Hat' was so important-so the Fashion Right Handbag was too – a mannequin often had one hung on her arm – so this was a 'Fashion Tale which they well knew. It concerned the spring shipments of fine leather bags from Milch. The timing was perfect – the wives of prominent judges and lawyers (the cream of the social scene you might say) – it was their spring luncheon meeting day at the Country Club not far away! They had been alerted 'they must stop and shop' we all eagerly watched for them – as the first few came thru the door – one hurriedly ran to the small beige satin stripe Settee- and Dumped the Entire Contents of her Handbag for All the World to see -! Compact – Lipstick – Cigarette – Case and Lighter Too – them something rather slim – sleek – silver and shiny came into view – a bit of a shock – quite a surprise – never seen before by my still naïve eyes a Ladies Elegant FLASK – you must remember the state was then still DRY! I learned many women wanted a NIP- A- SIP at lunch – and as the games of bridge and mahjongg went on perhaps a Bit More! So Much I learned in that Very First Store! As I dressed and re-dressed the Mannequins MORE and MORE – I called it FASHION-OSMOSIS – as from them I gained and gleaned MUCH FASHION LORE! In the years soon thereafter –'Prohibition' ended – our state went WET- perhaps that had a bit to do with the next trend in the handbag world – the smaller bag was demanded MUCH and next we saw the great popularity of the smaller bag called the CLUTCH! The third of the 'Famous Firsts' learned early on – observed that first month of March – In the Hour – Before the 'Monday morning unlocking of the store door – the mannequins saw a Sight on the Sidewalk – not as yet quite Witnessed Before! Waiting outside the door a small group – usually four – of Smiling – Giggly – Somewhat Shapely and rather Sexy young women! Each a crisp fresh $100 dollar bill did Hold – tightly between thumb and forefinger

Did Enfold – this the Mannequins and I overheard was the 'bit of Financial Treasure they had been paid for perhaps a 'Bit of Weekend Pleasure'! Paid for and enjoyed by their 'Sugar Daddies' Gentlemen in Oil or State Government's 'High Places' – men who wished to be Sure that they left no Loose Talk' or 'Tell Tale Traces' of their Indiscretions in 'Hidden Away Hotel Rooms' or Similar 'Secret Places'! These young women – never shy – were there to Buy New rather 'Lacy and Racy Lingerie' – To be ready for their Next Weekend of 'Pay for Play'! Seeking a Peek on a Monday – behind each other's 'Fitting Room Doors! They had No Interest in the 'Dinner Dresses' I sold – Early On – I was told 'Room Service Only' – Dull Dining In – That seemed to Be the 'Price Paid' with a crisp $100 dollar bill for a Young Lady Living Her Weekend In Sin!

Chapter III

Mannequins Their New Name Came
On a Warm Summer Day
How It was Given – Forevermore to Stay!

Mannequins – I learned early on could vary greatly in "Shape and Size" Earlier I had mentioned great differences often in their Eyes and Wigs could be changed 'On A Whim' Covering a 'Painted – On Hairstyle that remained underneath all the while – There were days I sometimes felt there were surely Eyes too 'In the Back of Their Heads' Otherwise how could they view – yes, they always knew – exactly what happened towards the back of the store of course 'Behind the Fitting Room Door'! The wonderful window mannequins – that I was so blessed to dress were basically slim of torso – long leg – we could call them – model-like – and tall. That first summer – as the weather became warm – I would become better acquainted with a shorter – more voluptuous – 'Torso Form'! Perfect for swimwear display on a hot summer day – I built not in the window, but on the floor – just inside the door of the store – 'Soak Up Some Sun' – 'Get an Even Tan' that was how every woman's swimsuit need began! – But the subject of 'Skin Cancer' or 'Danger from the Sun's Rays' were words I never heard 'Back in that Day'! Thus my challenge – with a bosomy torso model or two! Create 'A Seaside Setting'- see what I could do! The favorite swimsuit style – shiny – shimmering satin LASTEX – One Piece the Shades Most in Demand – pristine White – sunny Yellow or sleek shimmering Black – the provocative mannequin rested at floor level on a square of glass – admired by all who slowly passed – to create – in store – a touch of 'Seaside by the Shore'. A sprinkling of sand – assorted shapes and sizes of seashells – a beach bag and draped fishnet – no Flip Flops- they were not even heard of yet! I was admiring my 'Work of Swimwear Art' when suddenly came through the store door an excited pair of Pigtailed Precious 4-year-old Twins! I knew them and their mother well and quickly with urgency did tell "please let's be very careful of the Mannequin Display Today!" one twin tossed her head and rather questionably looked straight at ME – her hands on her childlike hips and these exact words came from her lips – a name forevermore to stay – "SHE is NOT a MANNEQUIN – SHE is a WomanAKIN CAN'T you SEE!" And the Name Remained the Same Evermore For ME!

Chapter IV

Now as Store Locations Changed
I Moved too – 4 Different Stores in
50 Years Surrounded by Changes of Title
– but Always on N. May Ave-

Chapter III ended with the official change of name from 'Mannequin' to 'WomenAKIN'! I was soon to realize it meant a bit of change also for me! Chapters I – II – with the 'Mannequins' were filled with laughter – fun and frivolity – the writing and words – left Always to Me. When 'WOMAN' a part of their title name became. They began to think as we Women so often do – they would not be content with just the First Word heard but expected to have the Last Word Too! An early thought they did convey to me – with 4 store locations in 50 years – I would be making and writing some 'Fashion History'! A word they didn't just suggest but strongly stressed was always PRIVACY – certain things must remain Forever a Mystery! NAMES not to be spoken or written in any form- names of owners stores – customers or future store locations – the first address I have already shared but from now on PRIVACY will prevail! You, the readers will just keep on 'guessing' as we share this 'N. May Fashion Tale! My titles I had several- the many decades' thru – titles which I shall share with you. But for a moment I shall digress and tell you the tale of a title that lasted at best an hour or two! Briefly bestowed upon me many years ago- by a slightly 'TIPSY' mother who came into the store where I was working with her young teen daughter in tow – this is how it did go! Wagging her Finger in the Faces of her Daughter and Me- 'you are here to

Find a Dress and you are going to be Helped by the 'MANAGERESS' she knows exactly what to do and she will Take Good Care of You'. Fortunately, we found a Dress – seemingly Pleasing to One and All- but that title I felt was not Befitting Me at All! In the 50 year span- various titles that I knew- various titles – I shall now share with you- Store Manager, Buyer – always Salesperson and Fashion Coordinator too- which entailed producing- outfitting models- writing and presenting our much – in-demand – Fashion Shows – often booked a year in advance – which I so LOVED to do! Last – But not Least – the title of 'WINDOW DRESSER' too – without which the 'WomenAKIN' and I would not have this our Fashion Tale to Share with You! Although the title of 'MANAGERESS' lasted only a mere hour or 2 – oh the Laughter it did evoke among the Fashion Folk – all the years of my stay on N. May Ave! Four stores in 50 years – so much joy and laughter – so few tears! A vow of privacy I did make so I shall define the stores only by the numbers of years in a location spent – and the number of ownership changes – should it apply. The first on N. May Ave its number of years (1961-63) 3 different owners in 2 years. The second store – (1963-69) always the same owner. The third store (1970-87) 2 different owners in 17 years. The fourth and final store (1987-2012) always the same owner 25 years!

Always moving farther north always on North May so thankful that I had 'Windows of ever- wonderful WomenAKIN' to Share and Care with Me All the Way!

Chapter V

*Fashion Shows Always Exciting and New
Fashion Shows Always Fun To Do And
View*

The 'Window WomenAKIN' always observed Me outfitting Fashion Show Models and always waited eagerly for me to regale them afterward with many a 'Fashion Tale' as to How it All Went! Long Years ago they chose to hear over and over of 2 shows that I CHOSE to do in the GREAT OUTDOORS! The First involved a Prominent Group of Politically Involved Women who opted to do a "Brunch" that began in the 'Cool of Morning' and went on to the Heat of the Noon Day Sun! It was held on the grounds of a Palatial Estate on the far edge of the city. Massive trees shaded the site and the Swimming Pool was unique and beyond compare! It also offered a very Elegant Pool House with plenty of dressing space for the models. I was informed that 'special walkways' were being erected so that the models might appear to be ' walking on the water' and that the large group of women seated poolside might better view the Glorious Groups of Summer Fashions chosen as being especially very 'colorful and new!' I was told many things in advance concerning the show but the one thing I Did Not Know was How Much in the Way of Alcoholic Beverages would flow in the Bar in the Dressing Area! Some models were 'tottering a bit' some were 'slightly soused' – as I uttered many a 'Fashion Word' fortunately the sound of 'SPLASH' was never heard! The models and their garments all remained 'DRY' and 'No Alcohol in the Dressing Room Please' became a rule that I asked that all 'Future

Fashion Shows Live By!' Another very popular fashion show was staged annually by 'Okla City Panhellenic' that young college girls might be 'in the know' as to how to dress for what was then called 'Rush Week' (Now they no longer go through RUSH it is called RECRUITMENT – sounds a bit like the military and NOT nearly as much FUN). Nonetheless, I shall share a 'Fashion Tale' as to how long ago the summer show once was done! The WomenAKIN were excited ' they had seen the young women being outfitted. On that beautiful summer evening, it was obvious that the show was going to outgrow its lovely indoor location (near the fairgrounds) and must overflow to the 'Great Outdoors.' I Did so Hope and Pray Before the show got underway that all would go well! The show was almost halfway thru when there came a 'shift in the wind' and the SMELL – the Aroma from the Stockyards was Blowing In! All at once out of the corner of my eye – I did spy a 'flock of pigeons flying by' somehow diverted in their flight by the sight of a Lovely and Loaded Refreshment Table – they Swooped Low and Over the Table Did Go – Marking their trail to no one's Taste or Sight Delight! The Fashion Show – a 'Feast For the Fashion Eye' but the Gourmet Goodies were left 'NOT EDIBLE' after the Pigeons Did Their Fly-By!

Chapter VI

Shoplifting – Gypsies – Teens – A Bank
Officer Too
Each Category Tried It's True
On North May Ave – the WomenAKIN
Knew Their Stories well – Thru the Years
These Shoplifter stories – often they did tell!
Now there were those who chose to shop
with EMPTY Pockets – Purses and Bags.
The ever – present shoplifting traffic – single
or in groups – would choose a store where
they could Park at the Door – Lift Their
Chosen Take and a 'Quick Getaway Make!'
Before 'My Day' and NOT on N.May – this
is a story of a Tragic Incident still Told!
Three 'Shoplifters and their Stash' made to
their 'Curbside Car a Dash and a beautiful

young store manager followed them out the door – hoping her merchandise to save – instead, she became hung on their Car's Fender – she was Dragged a Block or More – Sadly much too Early to Her Grave! Thus, to my co-workers I did stress – 'we Never Follow a Shoplifter Out the Door of the Store.' If a shoplifter was observed with merchandise and past the 'checkout counter' I would ask that they Quietly and Quickly Leave the Merchandise with Me – leave the store and Return No More! In that Day – no Guards or Security in shops along N. May – Of course some always did manage to 'Conceal and Steal' – In one case A Confession – A Change of Heart – A full Decade Later – It all Did End on a Busy Saturday – just as it had started on the Selling Floor of the very Same Store so Many Years Before! It was a spring Saturday before Easter that the WomenAKIN observed the final chapter unfold – Women of every age were there to Buy – the fitting rooms full – I was helping a Dr's wife – a cruise had come up as a surprise – she needed clothes and so it goes – a woman came into the store and Needed to See and Talk to Only Me – thus she waited an hour – until I was Free – Finally – at last – we went into my office and the story was told. Long years before she and her 'high school sweetheart' came into the store – between the 2 – no money – no funds at all – Spring Break she indeed a swimsuit did need! And there they saw a low rack of 'So New Bikini Swimwear' – 2 small pieces on a small clip hanger – he was wearing his 'Letterman's Leather Jacket' – he dropped to the floor – put a piece in each pocket in less than a minute it all was done – and she was ready that long past summer – to catch some Fun in the Sun. With Tears in her Eyes she took one of My Hands – with the Other Hand she Opened her Soft Pouchy Purse filled with Dollar Bills in all Denominations – 1s – 5s – 20s – 10s – Just say how much she said "I am here to make Amends" – I recently came to know the Lord in a very Personal Way – I feel led to Repay Merchants that I Shoplifted From. You and I are Doing That Today! As she sobbed I began to Pray – so Thankful for all that she was Experiencing – Peace and Forgiveness That Day. – She said Some Other Merchants took the Money – Gave Her a Look of Disdain which left Her still Feeling Guilt and Pain. I gave her an Approximate Swimsuit Prices back then – sealed the cash in an Envelope with the Owner's Name – a Christian gentleman – we Prayed again and closed it all with a final AMEN! One of the annual 'Rites of Spring' would – Be on N. May – the call of urgency the Gypsies are Coming Your Way' – 'Quickly – Lock the Doors' – Call the neighbors that they may Secure their Stores, But before all this "Forewarning came into play' it all came to pass this way on N. May! All Generations of Gypsies – all ages – poured out of their 'Dirty Dingy Dinged Vans' sometimes 1 often 2 – the children first thru the store door – they knew just what to do – Climb immediately into the windows 1 or 2 – the kids – 3 – 4 – or more WomenAKINS would have No Idea What To Do! – Divert the store staff – the Kids Tearing apart the window display – I well Remember Just Such a Day! One of the gypsies always cried – "I'm pregnant" – So Sick – the Restroom, she did Need – Several ran to the back always to try to 'lift' from 'Back Stock' and the Garments on the Layaway Rack! Each Gypsy bus or van had its own 'Quick Change Man' Waving a $ 20 dollar bill – in hopes to catch a glimpse of the Cash Register Till – and confuse the clerk – who always knew NOT to make change for the 'Jerk'! Now the Gypsies were obvious – Easy to spot – But there was one Unforgettable Customer – Turned – Shoplifter who was NOT! I was recovering from surgery – not officially back in the store – But at lunch break time, I would slip into a quiet well-hidden area of the store selling floor – rest in a small chair – well hidden from customer view – one salesperson would be on the floor and the rest could relax and chat together behind the lunch room door. The salesperson had a customer and I noted a Customer that I well knew came – in a 50ish Woman Bank Officer from a branch bank further north on May. – WE had a New Store that had opened much closer to that location – I saw her walk to a far corner of the store an area of Beautiful Dresses – but not her size – Her size hung in area open to view – the next thing I knew she Dropped Quickly to the floor and stuffed the soft dress quickly into a large bag that she pulled from her big Tote Bag – the bag from an earlier purchase at the store bought from me several months before! I was in a – state of shock! I knew I must talk immediately by phone to our further North May Ave store – as I felt she was on her way to make a Speedy Exchange of size or seek a Cash Refund that Very Day. I called the manager – who I had hired and trained for her job – that she was Not to Confront Her In Any Way – just merely say – 'Please Leave the Dress Today as we have No Sales Ticket to Show How it was Purchased (she said it was a gift) she wanted a Cash Refund – she was to leave her name and number – the store would be in touch – when she was called and told that 'unit control' showed the Dress had NEVER been Sold! The manager said that ended their conversation by phone. We had our merchandise and she had a 'shoplifting lesson' learned I never saw her again – within a month she had resigned her bank position and joined a bank out of state – this story of course, until now the WomenAKIN and I never shared for her 'Good Reputation' I so much Cared Her Reputation Remained Intact – and we Got Our Dress Back – a Shoplifting Lesson well learned! Behind the Fitting Room Door!

Chapter VII

To Market – To Market
Big Fashion News – the
YOUTHQUAKE
Is Coming – DENIM BLUES and
FADED too!

To Market To Market, I Must Go – Off to the Dallas Fashion Market Show – to Buy! There I First Heard the Phrase Proclaiming the upcoming 'FASHION CRAZE'! 'The YOUTHQUAKE is Coming! Market was the place to Start to Buy for the YOUNG And those Merely YOUNG at Fashion Heart! "Skirts Had Never Been Shorter" Everywhere one looked – one did see More Than Just A Peek Above the Knee'. For the

young it was FUN – Most looked well –
Sorry but in the Older Gals – KNEES Didn't
Really Look so SWELL! But – For Me and
the Store I was In At the Time – It all Really
Did Turnout Fine! It was the Era of 'In Store
Personal Charge accounts' That amounts to
Both Mother and Daughter – 'On the
account might BUY – And some New Ideas
I Did Try! 'A Sugar 'n Spice Corner' with
Everything Nice for Girls!' Fashions for the
Young were NEW – Tastefully chosen
Fashion and Tasty Sweet and Sugary
TREATS in Abundance too! Suddenly
cotton DENIM in blues became the Biggest
Fashion NEWS – But we needed to avoid the
Fade and the Mess the Ruboff Dye made – So
it came time for Pre Wash Denim to answer
the 'Fashion Call' And for every Age and
Stage of Denim wearer that Solved it ALL!
Cotton denim in white 'Caught on Too' –
But nothing would Ever Outsell the Blue
Denim for Daytime and into the Evening
Too. – Rhinestone and Sequins all at once –

many Sparkles to View! Today we would call it 'BLING' – But at that time, as I earlier said, the word 'BLING' had not as yet been Heard! Every Jean Hip Pocket was all at once Worn with Special Adornment! A Fashion Hit on the Hip – Denim skirts too – Sometimes Full often Slim – Denim Shirts and Jackets 'All Were In' – The 'YOUTHQUAKE' what a huge difference in the Purchasing Power of the Young it Would Make! – It was a Time – Shortly before there were Enclosed malls to Entice – so I Must Make the Store I Managed Offer More to Bring Teens Through the Door – more than simply 'sugar 'n spice'! – Happily my new concept – In Store Sub-Deb Fashion Education 'worked out very well – The size of the Saturday Morning in-store Classes began to swell! The girls attending chatted and often during the week would sneak in to take a peek – view what was new – and check with their moms to see if 'A Layaway They Might Do?!' On Saturday they learned how to choose what was Fun and Flattering as well as Hints on various aspects of 'Charm – Makeup – Modeling – Manners – and Etiquette too' How extremely fortunate and blest I was – to have teaching with me a former 'Miss Oklahoma' she was also a finalist for 'Miss America' too! Our Sub-Deb Charm and Fashion Education 'Graduations' were Done in This Way. – At a country club long gone Today – At a Sunday evening 'Dinner and Dance Soiree – After the Buffet was cleared away and before the Dancers took over the floor – I took over the microphone for a 'Teen Fashion Scene' Fashion Show and Presentation of the 'Charming Young Sub-Deb Models. They walked a Ramp and showed Darling Clothes and Then as the Excitement Grows – All at once the music slows – as each Deb's name I Did Read – She Stepped Down from the Stage – Her Proud Father was waiting between the Stage and the Band to take Her Proudly by the Hand – onto the Dance Floor – Their Picture snapped – 'A Memory

Visually and in Heart Captured – To be remembered Ever more!' But before we leave the 'YOUTHQUAKE' Sub-Debs and the 'Early Denim Teen Scene' There is a 'Fashion Tale' the WomenAKIN ask me to tell and retell. It concerned an Elegant Show I was asked to do – A few years Before much was voiced 'Fashionably about Denim Blue!' – But nonetheless quite unexpectedly 'It became a part of THAT Show too'! Denim Blue – Wrinkled – Ripped and Rumpled and Roughly Worn – All at Once – FELL into Full View! Read on!

Chapter VIII

A Focus on the Long Ago Local Fashion Scene

–

First the Governor's Mansion Show –
Then to Two Fashion Book Reviews, We
Will Go!

Thank you for 'Reading On' as you were Instructed to Do! This chapter deals with fashion on the Long Past Local Scene. One the WomenAKIN love to hear me tell is this 'Fashion Show' Story from so Long Ago! The Governor's Mansion was the scene and a Fabulous Showing of Fall Fashions There Would Be Seen. Fashion pieces available Locally and Exceptionally Elegant Furs and Jewelry Pieces had All Just Arrived by Air

from New York City for the Large
Assembled Group of Fashionable Ladies to
View! The Models would enter down the
Beautiful Staircase from the second floor of
the Governor's Mansion. Several Security
Guards were stationed on two- watching
over the Furs and Sparkling Stone Set Jewelry
Pieces too. Now a 'Fashion Shade' that season
receiving much acclaim was 'Bottle Green'
by name. In a state so long DRY. the shade of
a rich, deep green wine bottle really 'caught
the eye'! I stood at the foot of the Staircase
by the Newel Post. Looking up at the next
model – The most attractive wife of the 'then
mayor of OKC' was showing in fashion
terms a cocktail dress in Bottle Green
'Puckered Satin' a textured fabric new on the
fashion scene – her mini box style Cocktail
Handbag was richly encrusted rhinestone on
gold- I anticipated she would be followed
by a model wearing a 'Mink Stole Wrap' –
she wore Jewels of Glistening Gold and then
a true 'Fashion Show Nightmare!' Began to

Unfold. Somehow between Bottle Green Satin and Mink- There came THREE Young Teens – Screaming Barefoot Kids in Dirty Ragged JEANS Pushing Fighting came Tumbling Down the Stairs – Obviously I was Totally Unaware of What was Happening in another bedroom upstairs – It seems the Governor and his wife had been called unexpectedly out-of-state- their children had been told that 'Ladies would need their Rooms in which to Dress for Just a Little While'. Parents, away there was a real problem there and the Security Staff said they (the kids) really needed to go Downstairs (use the back stairway) but instead the kids got into a Hassle and Began to Push Shove and Wrestle – and Pell-Mell Down the Stairs They Fell – A gasp from the tea time ladies – I continued to Smile All the While- I stepped around them there at the Foot of the Stair – they scrambled out the closest door leaving me- only to Think of Commentary and the next Model Clad in Mink! Although it did not go off totally as I had Planned – I was told at its Close – that the Clothes and the Fact that I never 'Lost my Cool' made it a Fun Show to View and For the Most Part Quite GRAND!

On that occasion the show's malfunction and mishap was in 'Full View'- On other occasions there were Two Shows only I could Spy Out of the Corner of My Eye – the Fashion Foible that would soon unfold and eventually the Whole Audience Would Behold- these are also tales the WomenAKIN loved- well and said I should tell and retell – this First Story has a Bit of a 'SMELL'!

In that Era- so long ago- some 'Fashion Books' had been written and were being widely discussed- and it was decided (of course by ME) that I must begin to do what I would call a 'Fashion Book Review' No Models but rather 'A Fashion Display' Garments and Accessories- some hung on a folding screen other pieces on risers could be easily seen- The concepts in the book I could

clearly illustrate and refer to in the course of
the review- women found it 'new' and called
it 'great'. This is what I was set-up to do in a
very fashionable 'Basement Meeting Space'-
The Luncheon was over and my Review
about half thru as I turned from the Book to
point and gaze toward the Display. I thought
my 'eyes must be doing something strange
today' I thought I saw Something From The
Ceiling Drop – the Review I was Not About
To 'STOP'- a Speedy Conclusion and there
had been more Drops – on the ceiling there
was now forming a 'SPOT'- that Day I Saw
and I Did Smell – up close and personal what
it was like when Raw Sewerage thru the
lovely basement ceiling Fell and Sadly I Must
Tell – two Garments Spoiled Soiled – Ruined
beyond Repair – Yes, the Building
Management Did Cheerfully for Them Pay –
but neither they nor I would soon forget the
rather Costly and Smelly Review I Did Do
in their Basement that Day! The 2nd Event
I glimpsed – It was a Hot Sunny Day – a

posh country club where I would be doing a Different Review and Building a totally new Fashion Display! – A large group of women in town with their husbands for a golfing event looked forward to Luncheon and a Fashion Event- indoors and cool and yet able to see a view out over the green where in the distance their Husbands could be seen -. They were seated and their luncheon done – ready for some 'FASHION FUN' where I was standing I could see an archway and an adjoining room NOT in use that day – I am happy to say! – For some work was being done on the roof over that room that day – the extreme Heat outdoors the outside work- who could say? but Out of the Corner of my eye I did Spy that Day – Clean White Ceiling Material All At Once Quickly Give Away – no Smell of which to Tell – just Plaster Dust filled the Air! In the adjoining room – No Gloom nor Doom with Me in the Ballroom- I'm Happy to say- I remember it All So Well that Hot Sunny Fashion Review Day!

Chapter IX

As I Recall Fashion Memories Now Long Past
–

The Youthquake –
The Denim So Blue
Customer Friends –
Now I Have You – a 'New Reader' Friend,
Do You Happen to Recall – Let's all Read
on too–

Perhaps I Helped You with your Prom Dress? Yes, then In Store we did your Fashion Footwear too? The Prom and Pageant Dress – always required at that time – the Perfectly Dyed-to-Match Shoe! Even more important than just the right shade of shoe – no one ever at your Prom or Pageant would Dare show up Wearing the Same Dress as You! Notes on who bought which Dress – I started making months in advance – that there would never be the chance that I Might, that I might that Fatal Error- that Huge Great Fashion Mistake Make! – I must Never – Knowingly – Be a Part of the Greatest Kind of FASHION MESS – 2 Beautiful Young Women- Arriving Perhaps at An Elegant Holiday Ball – Arriving – Wearing the Very Same Dress – Would You Guess – Did It Ever Happen at All?!! My Precious Young Customer Friend Excited for Her Great Event – Arrived at a Much Anticipated Holiday Ball – the Band was already playing 'White Christmas' so to the Dance Floor they went! – Shock of shocks- It was the 'Dress Mess'- 2 Dresses Exactly the same- worn to the 'Christmas Ball'- of course being 'Holiday Red'- they were quickly Viewed and Observed by All!

My Darling Young Customer Friend Knew I Had One and Only One of THAT

DRESS in Stock- Especially for Her on This Occasion at Market I Had Bought! Soon I Learned The Other young lady and her mother to Dallas Had Flown – that her Dress Might be that Holiday Be – Hers and Hers Alone in OKC! I Heard that she Had Paid Far More – A Price Far Greater Than That Paid on N. May – Behind the Fitting Room Door!

A Thought One Day on which I Paused and Did Dwell – As there could be a 'Dress Mess' in Life – There could be a 'Same Dress Mess' in Death – For all Eternity!

As the Years and Beloved Customer Friends Passed On, More and more Families turned to Me – How Would a Cherished Mother- Grandmother – Great Grandmother have Chosen to be 'Viewed'-? Perhaps in her Favorite Shade – Color on Hue and Always A Flattering Neckline Too! Perhaps Rather Than Choosing something 'New' A Daughter – Niece or Dear Friend Might Go to the Closet of the Deceased Make the Choice – I would never know?! These were

Ladies I Had Lovingly Been Blest to Dress- the Decades Thru- Often in a week I might Lose 1 or 2 and in the same Funeral Home they were listed as 'on view'- After Church on a Sunday I would hear my Husband say – "Do We Need to Make the 'Funeral Home Fashion Run' Today"? As this story Ends I share with You – an Episode I Recall as True – Only Part-time was I working – each week- 3 Days – the others I spent in Tulsa – my Mother – terminally ill there-. Home on Sunday – By the Funeral Home- yes I wished to Go! On My Visiting I was Relieved to see- 2 Ladies Who had been as 'Dear, Customer Friends' for many a year – Each a Beautiful Dress wore – yes, they were from the Store – But I Had, my Store Angels – in training they had learned well – Best Friends Should Not Be Shown the SAME Dress as a Friend Perhaps had Bought – even in a different shade – this was Not The Thing to Do! To the Best of My Knowledge, no one Did Ever See – Concurrently – two Ladies Behind

'Neighboring Slumber Room Doors' Dressed alike To Be a 'Fashion Mess' – For All Eternity! Let them always be Laid to Rest in the Color in Life they Wore Best!

Always the ever aware WomenAKIN and I Did Try so hard to AVOID 'SAME DRESS MESS!' Before we leave the subject- Best to Mention Now With You – The Basic Little Black Dress – The Ever -Versatile Black Suit too-

So similar – Could Be Called 'Look Alike Too'- Remember It's always How You Choose to Accessorize that Makes It Very Personally You! – Perhaps Jewelry- a Scarf – Shawl – or a Jacket You chose? – Maybe something as 'Sheer and Striking' as your Legs Showing off a pair of Patterned or Textured Hose! Enjoy Your choice of the Basic Little Dress – Change It in Many Ways and make it ever reflect your 'Good Taste'- If in your closet there is not ONE hanging there – then in HASTE put it on your 'TO

BUY LIST' there is not a Shopping Moment
to WASTE!

Chapter X

Fashion World Proves to be More and
More –
A Reflection of World Events as well as
"Goings On'
Just Outside the North May Avenue
Fitting Room Door' Sonic Booms and MORE

Over the World – Decades Thru -there
were wars and 'Rumors of Wars'. Once
more a Reflection on the 'Fashion Scene'
Fabrics and Printed Fabric what will it all
mean?- It meant more and more pieces
in cotton were seen! Sometimes slacks and
suits in shades of Military Tan and Khaki too
– uniquely styled and shaded – yes, it is true –

Camouflage Prints' big time came into view -!

Looking back I recalled the 'not so fashionable' influence of the 'Flower Children' and 'Hippies too' – Briefly They Did All Pass Thru – None enjoyed 'too long a stay' on the Fashionably correct 'Ave' of N. May!

Assassinations – Changes in the White House – New 'First Ladies' in Fashion Full View – No woman of that time will ever forget the day when the Ever-Elegant Jackie Kennedy was so quickly and tragically whisked away in the Rose-Shaded Blood Spattered Suit she was Wearing in Dallas That Assassination Day – Her little – so Fashion Right Pill Box Hat Never Askew – as Scrambling Secret Service Agents tried Hard to Hide the 'Horror' from the World's Eyes on Live TV News View! You who were Alive that Day- Remember that Heart-Breaking Happening in your 'Mind's Eye' as if it Might Have Been Only Yesterday.

The World was still reeling from the Shock of it all – So too was it on N. May Ave. Customers Remained at Home to Watch the Funeral Procession Move By. As so small – young Son John Jr. Saluted – there was scarcely a Dry Eye! Customer Friends were not out to Visit – Browse or Buy! This Time of Grief would not be Brief!. The Tragedy of it all – over the Nation Seemed to Have 'Cast a Pall'-. The owner of the Store at that time was a very quiet genteel Lady – We sat in the store – not a customer in sight–just the WomenAKIN under the ever Glaring Window Light.

Suddenly thru the Door of the Store – A Rather Pushy- Bombastic Salesman Came – A Road Rep we knew all too well- Both by Reputation and By Name! The owner in her ever kind way told him she would be at Market Soon and was NOT 'OPEN to Buy' that afternoon – He left – several minutes passed by – and the next thing we knew He was pushing open the Door – Rolling a

Loaded Rack of Sample Garments into the Store! The owner remained unruffled and calm and repeated her earlier phrase – one well known in the trade- "I am sorry But I am not 'Open to Buy Today". Grumbling He Pushed the Rack back to the Door – His Final Words – I Heard Him say – 'You two just aren't BITCHY Enough to SUCCEED in 'This Business' Anyway! And still, Today I have to Consider that a Compliment – in a Strange Way! The Business went on Most Successfully for Many a Year'-

While World Events – Shook us to our 'Fashion Core'- One Summer we were shaken 'Sky High', each Day at precisely 12:00 o'clock – High Noon, we were shaken by the SONIC BOOM – the store windows in place – would slightly sway – Had the WomanAKIN had Hearts – they would have been Beating Faster! I urged customers to move to the Back of the Store – perhaps Behind A Fitting Room Door- in case there just might be – a store window 'Shattered

Glass Disaster' – Thankfully That We Never Did See!

But sadly a story that must here be told – As Nature's Wrath in the form of a True Tornado and Traumatic Winds did once unfold! I left the store at closing all was safe as I locked the door – Early Evening – a Suddenly Strange and Sudden Storm Darkened the Sky – not just Traumatic Winds but a True TORNADO came Tunneling and Funneling Thru in all of its Howling Horror Leaving Spots of Retail in Ruins along N. May Ave. 'Small Strip Shops' virtually 'Blown Away'- the Store I had left so shortly before in a Matter of Hours was No More – the Top Layer of the Roof was Totally Blown Away and before projected rain storms were headed that way – May Ave was by 'the OKC Police Force brought by Barricades to a Quick Close – Only Business Owners were allowed thru – Salvaging Merchandise to any Storage Areas – As the next day dawned the owner and I set out to view – what might be readily available for 'immediate occupancy' and my in-store life moved ever – successfully undaunted by Tornadic Trauma ever – further north on May Ave – A Happy Ending to a Fashion Horror Story – And behind the new store window More NEW WomenAKIN came immediately Fashionably Dressed into Full View!

Before this chapter's closing the WomenAKIN who had lived 'window-wise'- thru the summer of the SONIC BOOMS – thought the readers should know 'Why the 'SONIC BOOM' tests and What They Did Show? – Factually – Over 50 years ago – these Daily Tests were Conducted Over OKC by the U.S. Air Force and the FAA with this question – 'Could a City Continue to Function Normally with 'Supersonic Transportation' involving 'Super Fast' Planes that were known to produce 'SONIC BOOM SOUNDS-?' No Final Word Found – After a Summer of SONIC

BOOM Sounds – I shall merely say – OKC
continues to Function Normally – Alive and
Well – to this VERY DAY!

Chapter XI

Economic BOOMS
– Busts and More Women Out the Door –
Playing Evermore Roles in Career
– Community and Family –
Dressing for Success in the Workplace or
the next 10K Race!

Just as 'SONIC BOOM' Reverberations were felt both Near and Far Away So too was there a Time when the terms 'OIL BOOM and BUST' affected Our Economy both Near and Far – and Especially on N. May – for we in the 'Fashion Field' heard whispered 'Behind the Fitting Room Door'- as well as on the 'Sales Floor'- Words such as these – A Very New Need- Fashion Wise Women were thinking 'Career Wise'-! Not only a 'Paycheck' did they Seek but a Change in their Status as Women'! We the women who have lived thru World War II – were often better educated than the Women Who Made Up the Generation Before – Still, we were feeling the need to see a 'post-war Husband Degreed'- the Babies Came and As they Grew- All of Volunteerism needed Our Time and Talents Too!

The Late Great Erma Bombeck created for us a Name – one that attributed to her much too short-lived- but much loved and well-remembered fame! The Term- 'Justa Housewife'- Our Talents – Countless in Number – Performed Often and Perfected Well -! We were the women who in addition to being Wives, Mothers and always Church and involved Community Volunteers – heard a phrase that was 'music to our ears' – we were so many Women Seeking NEW CAREERS – and thru the years as our Careers began to Progress –

perhaps it was Because We Tended To Believe That In Order to Succeed – we needed to 'Dress For Success' – While still often playing the wife and mother roles too – perhaps having once been 'Justa Housewife' multitasking was Something we had Really Learned to Do !

In addition to all the rest we learned the Importance of Health- Mind Body and Spirit – all seemed to be Equally Important too. Thus Women Began to Walk, to Run – Exercise – Before or After The Work Day – which led to a Need for Exercise Wear – Women could Find It in a small shop on N. May – Something to Wear while Running the Much Discussed Upcoming 10K!?

More and More Women Out the Door – For Career – For Health – For Pleasure and Family Fun – and the WomenAKIN and I Learned that Fashion – continued Ever and seasonally Changing – I once compared it again to a 'Kaleidoscopic View' – Ever

Changing – Ever New – Ever Exciting and Beautiful to View!

In My 'Fashion Lifetime' Behind the Fitting Room Door – and 'Ever further Northward on N. May'- I did see Innovations that Meant Much to Me and Those I was so Privileged to call My 'Customer Friends'- before this chapter on Our Booming and Blooming Status of Women ends – Four Changes – First Women's Buying Power Grew – Second In the Career World there was Greater Self-Esteem and Self-Worth Gained – The Final Two – A Woman Could Securely Hold 'One in Each Hand' – A Charge Card in Her Own Name and Panty Hose – Never Again Need a Crooked Stocking Seam Be Seen!

There was a quick window dressing change of garment one day and a WomanAKIN repeated a phrase she heard a woman say – that day- it was spoken to a Shopping friend – simply 'We've come a Long Way Baby' – the WomanAKIN wondered if I thought that was True? And I Was More Convinced Each Day I Spent On May Ave – and Happy to Say – 'You Bet I Do' So True – We've Come a Long Way Baby! You and I Too!

Chapter XII

Thankful for Many Lessons Learned From
– Angel Co-Workers Customer Friends
Too –
As I grow older – Hopefully Wiser on N.
May Ave.

In over 50 years – Half a Century – Lived out on N. May – There We Met Needs That Were Constant Decade After Decade – Day after Day – Yes, Baby We as Women Did Come a Long Way! As this Fashion Tale seems to go without End – Events and Experiences All Seem to Rather Blend – Alone, I would Never Be – Before Opening the Door of the Very First Store, I Asked Prayerfully that the Lord Be With Me That

Day, and All Along the Way- I'm sure the Lord Knew from His View of Eternity – Although for Him Brief, It seemed to Be – A long Journey as it Loomed Ahead for A Mere Mortal Such as Me – Not by Accident But 'Heaven Sent' – My Co-Workers I Called 'Angels' – They Flew from Fitting Room to Fitting Room – Day by Day – Meeting the Needs of Our "Customer Friends' – in a Most 'Heavenly Way' – No Commissions were Ever Made – No 'Push Money' ever Paid – But a Generous 'Merchandise Discount' in the store We were Allowed and a Flexible Work Schedule for my Angelic Co-Workers I always Vowed to Do. Example – 'Mommy Hours' if wanted – I would Do – When the last child in the Morning was out the door – Come for 'Fashion Work And Fun' in the Store! But Be Back at Home when the Kids come Home at the School Day's End. Happily, there always seemed to be Fashion-wise' teens and plenty of eager DECA trained girls waiting and watching the clock for their 'Work Day' to Begin – They loved Weekend and extra Holiday Hours Best – A Win-Win For Me! With Happy Working Store Angels, I was Always Blest and No Church Camp or Summer Vacation Trip was Ever to Be Missed! Always an – Angel Could Fly – In to Fill In From My Large 'Waiting List'!

Only recently I Heard a Younger Man Say – "I remember when I was just a 'little guy' – I got sick at school one day – My mom worked with you in the store in N. May- She picked me up and suddenly I felt BETTER – and you had a corner in the store where I Might Rest and Stay and Play- and my Divorced Mom might finish out those valued 'Hours of Her Mommy Work Day' without losing any Pay!" Still – No High 'Hourly Wage – Commission or 'Push Money' Paid – My goal There was There Be an Atmosphere of Christian Warmth – Love and Concern for other 'Angels' – and Customer Friends Feel the Camaraderie – And I Knew – So

True – it must 'ever Begin With Me'! – For Something More than Just 'Body Cover' or 'New to Put on to Wear' – So often our Customer Friends were there with Problems – Traumas both Large and Small – Did They need a Hand to Clasp – A Listening Ear – A Heart-Warming Word of Prayer to Share? An Incident 'Ever to Remain with Me – Permanently Etched in Brain and Memory – It Began Like Any other Day on N. May- And By Afternoon Busy – So many Fashion Shows To Do – I Recall I Had 'Models' that were Breast Cancer Survivors for the Annual "Especially For You" Show – So Long – I Really Don't Know – they may have been from the Geology Wives Show – Today I Cannot Say! In the Midst of it All, A Precious Customer Friend 'dropped in' – Very, very Seldom Could She Afford to Buy – She Liked to See 'What was New' and on Leaving Always wished to Share a 'Hug or Two'! So Busy that Day – No more than a Quick Glance – A Wave and a Smile We Did Share

– I'm Haunted Still Today – Might it All
Have Turned Out Some Other Way If I had
only Had a Minute to Spare that Day!
Quickly, She Chose a Lovely Dress – the
'Angel' who Had Assisted Her Said She Did
Not Wish to 'Try it On' – When I looked
up again- She Had Purchased, Paid in Cash
and so Quickly She was GONE! Less than
a Week Passed and quite Shockingly a Brief
Notice of Her Death I Did See – No
Mention of a Funeral or Full Obituary!
Another Few Days and I Did Behold A
Gentleman – Carrying that 'Lovely Dress' so
Recently Sold – He wore a Bit of a Frown
– As He Almost Threw it Down on the
Counter by the Cash Register – I Hear Him
Say – 'It Was a Cash Sale – Never Worn –
" I'd Like My Money BACK TODAY!" Had
His Dear Late Wife Been Thinking Suicide
That Day? And was this the Garment in
which She Had Chosen to Be Laid Away?
Another Question – the Answer to Which
Would Remain Unknown – Would the

Story Have Ended Differently – If that Day I might not so BUSY had been – When She Came in With a 'Load of Care' and Perhaps a Burden She Had Wished to Share – Perhaps if I Had Been There Free To Suggest A Moment or Two of PRAYER? For I Know in My 'Heart of Hearts' Lord, You are There Just as You Had Said You Would Be – Waiting Near with a Listening Ear – Attuned to Hear My Every Prayer – Thankfully I Remain Forever Near Dear Lord to Thee!

Chapter XIII

And Thankfully Two Days Later
– It Was a Saturday and That Was The
Day –
the WomenAKIN Told Me It Was Time to
Pray and Share
– To Affirm The Fact That They and I
Always Knew To Be True
– Before I Went Through The Door of
That First Elegant Store
– That The Lord Continues to
MIGHTILY Be With Me
– That Day and All the Days – Be They
Many or Few–
Behind the Fitting Room Door on N. May
Ave –

It was far less than half way – thru my Fashion Journey on N. May Ave – that in the last hour before closing that Saturday as the Angels and I were doing some straightening – it had been a Busy Sale Day I heard myself say – I'm Coming In an Hour Before We Open for Business on Monday – More and More Needs Seem Daily To Be Shared – if any of You are Scheduled on Monday – I'll Be In Front Near The Counter With Some Chairs – The Door Will Be Unlocked.

I Remember So Joyfully I Was Shocked as NOT Only The Co-Workers Were There Too – but one brought a neighbor who indeed felt the Need for Shared Prayer Before Beginning a New Uncertain Week too! The Store in Early Morning Peace and Calm – not all the Glaring Overhead Lights Turned On – An Area Became a Place to Share a Prayer and Pray – In the Weeks and Months that Followed – Workers from Stores up and down the block – Came with Needs and to 'Prayerfully Talk' – Cancer – Divorce – In

Those Days not as much heard of Drugs and Addiction and Today's ever rising Alzheimer's Affliction – War and Rumors of War – then and now were heard too. Our Needs and Numbers in Weeks Ever Grew – Shared Prayer There as We Began each Monday with a Brief Scripture Reading and a Bible Verse or two. God's Word Became More ALIVE – Did our Businesses Thrive and Prosper in any way? Today I Don't Recall – but 'Riches and Rewards' in Our Lives – not Measured in a Monetary Way – Came Our Way in a Warm and Caring Way – Just as I had said I Always Wanted It to Be- among my 'angels' an ever-growing Camaraderie! Then and Now My Needs You Always Seem To Know – and Now My Aging Needs Seem Ever To Grow! If I Just Reach Out to YOU with my Morning Prayer – Dear Lord you take my Hand and Safely Guide my Faltering Steps into Each New Day!

I am No Longer on N. May but I Live

Now Just A Few Short Blocks Away. No more WORDS – Heard although Unspoken, from My WomenAKIN on N. May – But My Bond With Them – As With YOU Lord Created in a Time So Long Past – Shall Forever Last – Forever and a Day Unbroken-

And as I arrive at 'Ninety' SOON- that Day of Heavenly Reunion May Not Be Too Far Away!

Perhaps NOW this "Little Book with its Many a Look – Behind the Fitting Room Door" – needs Nothing More than a One Word Closing – Honoring Our Simple and Shared Prayers That Seemingly Know No END – So I Shall Write – As I Simply Utter This Heartfelt Word of Closeness and Closure a Written and Whispered AMEN- Dear Reader Friend.

Epilogue

With a Prologue the years
'Behind the Fitting Room Door' Did Start

–

So perhaps for the 'Final Words' and '
Closing' an Epilogue might be Smart!

The WomenAKIN and I have Shared and YOU 'Dear Reader Friend' Have Patiently Read ON! From 'Little Miss Droopy Drawers' Bloomers – My 'Big Girl Panties' I Pulled Up and Moved On – Bikini Panties – yes, I Sold Many a Pair and Wore a Few Pair Too! NOW before my 'Time of Morning Prayer' I don my 'Incontinence Underwear'! My 'Prayer Time' – and On To Another Day – Still Just a Few Short Blocks Away From N. May Avenue!

79478697R00057

Made in the USA
Columbia, SC
27 October 2017